I AM SECOND®

# I AM SECOND®

## Real Stories. Changing Lives.

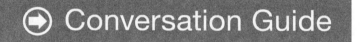
### Conversation Guide

## THOMAS NELSON
*Since 1798*

NASHVILLE  DALLAS  MEXICO CITY  RIO DE JANEIRO

Published in Nashville, Tennessee, by Thomas Nelson. Thomas Nelson is a registered trademark of Thomas Nelson, Inc.

Published in association with the literary agency of Wolgemuth & Associates, Inc.

Thomas Nelson, Inc., titles may be purchased in bulk for educational, business, fund-raising, or sales promotional use. For information, please e-mail SpecialMarkets@ThomasNelson.com.

ISBN: 978-1-4016-7580-6

*Printed in the United States of America*

12 13 14 15 16 QG 6 5 4 3 2 1

**Freedom. Love. Success. Happiness.**

Everyone is looking for something. Discover the stories of people who tried to find it. They tried to find it through drugs, pleasure, and money. But nothing worked. Nothing filled the hole in their chests. Relationships crumbled; the money just caused more problems; struggles and addictions riddled their lives. Nothing satisfied. That is, until they became Second, and that changed everything.

Be inspired by their stories. Be challenged by the lessons they teach. Learn to tell your own story. And discover for yourself the power of a life dedicated to Second.

# contents

# leader's guide

For training films, free downloads, and other bonus content, register at **iamsecond.com/bonuscontent**.

# before you start

Here are a few tips and pointers that will help keep this Second group the healthy, interactive, and life-changing community it is designed to be.

Go over these together:

## Who can join the group?

I Am Second groups are for anyone wanting to discover more about Jesus. If people are interested in learning more, in discovering the raw, authentic, and often challenging stories of real people becoming Second, then this group is for them. Be sensitive to the needs of the group when setting the time and place of the meetings.

## What can I expect?

Be sure each person in your group has a copy of this participant's guide and a copy of the book *I Am Second: Real Stories. Changing Lives*. Participants will use both resources extensively throughout each week.

## Two Stories

Each session contains two stories. The first story focuses on a contemporary issue and personality. Some of these people are famous; others are not. All of them are equally authentic. Before each session the group can read these stories in the book. Each session begins with a first-person retelling of the story through an I Am Second film.

The second story comes from the Bible. These stories show Jesus interacting with real people dealing with the same issues as the first story. The goal is to see how these ancient stories can bring new insights about life and about God.

Your group will learn from these stories by way of discussion. There is a series of open-ended questions for each story for your group to discuss.

## Live and Tell

At the end of every session are two questions. The Live and Tell questions are designed to help you obey and follow through with the things you learn. These stories are meant to inspire, challenge, and yes, even change everyone in the group. But for this change to happen, each person needs to seriously and specifically discuss what those changes should look like in his or her own life. The Live and Tell questions are designed to help you do just that. So be sure to not skip these vitally important questions.

## The Power of Story Session

The first session will be different from the other sessions. Rather than discussing a specific topic, your group will share and discuss your own I am Second stories. This discussion guide will touch on deep and personal topics, addictions, relationships, wealth, death, and more. In order for you to have the meaningful and personal discussions intended for your group, you will first need to know a bit about the background, experiences, struggles, and relationship with God that everyone in your group has had. This first session will set the relational foundation for your group to move forward in the rest of this discussion guide. To give you time to share and discuss your own I am Second stories, there will be no Bible story or Live and Tell for this first session.

## How do I keep the discussion going?

### Rule 1—Speak in Sentences, not Paragraphs

Let every person's voice be heard. There are times set aside throughout the course of this material that let all group members share their life stories, but in the normal course of your group, everyone's interactions should be short and to the point.

## Rule 2—No Topic Surfing

Focus on only one story and one Bible passage each meeting. Do not surf through other stories, other Bible passages, sermons, books, or outside sources that the rest of the group may not be familiar with. If the group discovers an I am Second story or Bible passage that everyone wants to discuss together, feel free and even encouraged to do so, but not right then. Schedule another meeting at another time.

# How does the Live and Tell work?

## Rule 3—Keep Externally Focused

The insights learned in this group are meant to be lived out and shared with the people in your lives. Things are supposed to change. If people leave the same way they entered, then this group has failed. Expect to be challenged. Expect to change. And be ready to share what is learned with friends and family.

## Rule 4—Challenging but Doable

Every Live and Tell commitment should be both challenging and doable. If someone was already planning on calling his or her dad that week, then committing to do it as the Live and Tell is not challenging. On the other hand, committing to call his or her dad and address every problem and issue they ever had is likely too challenging. So find a balance between these two extremes, and make every commitment both challenging and doable.

## Rule 5—Action, Date, Time

Make your Live and Tell commitments as specific as possible and be sure to write them down to help the group remember everyone's commitments. Maybe restoring a broken relationship with an old friend is someone's Live commitment, and a great commitment that would be. But what does that look like? What *action* will need to be taken to begin the restoration process? Do you need to call someone? Do you need to change a behavior? *When* will that action be done? Tomorrow? The day after? Will it be at work? During lunch? Work as a group to develop a specific action plan to actually live out what each person is learning. This will help everyone successfully implement the things they are learning in the group.

## Rule 6—Avoid "Sunday School" Answers

"I'll read my Bible more this week." "I'll pray more." "I'll memorize a verse." These may indeed be the right answers for someone. But before accepting one of these familiar responses, challenge people to ask if God might have something more specific for their lives that he wants them to commit to. Is there a relationship that needs healing, a struggle that needs dealing with, an action that needs doing in order to touch the lives around them?

## What if I'm not yet Second?

Regardless of religious background, everyone is still encouraged and challenged to participate in the Live and Tell. Some may choose not to participate. But I Am Second groups are action, oriented, and most will likely find that living out what they learn is an exciting and empowering experience.

## What's next?

Each week, you will be challenged to tell others what you are learning. Use this as an opportunity to find people interested in discussing spiritual things. At the end of this discussion guide, you will be challenged to consider starting a new group with the people in your life who are interested in experiencing the power of real stories and changing lives.

## Are there more resources for me and/or my church?

Yes. Register your group or church at **iamsecond.com /bonuscontent** and get access to group leader training films, free video downloads, and more.

# 1.0 the power of story

Be sure to review the "Before You Start" section before beginning.

**Introduction**: Spend a few minutes to take turns introducing yourselves to the group. What brought you to this group? What do you hope to discover through this group?

**Watch**: the Josh Hamilton or Michelle Aguilar film

**Talk about the film:**

1. What do you like about the story?

2. What do you not like or find confusing about the story?

3. What did you learn from the story?

## Your story

If you were sitting in the white chair, what would you say? Here are some topics you might talk about in your story:

⊙ What events or people brought you to a point where you were interested in spiritual things?

⊙ What are some important events from your life?

- Where are you with God now?
- How did you get to this place with God?
- What are some questions you still struggle with about life or God?

Be sure to save time for everyone to share their stories.

# Next Week—
# Second: Struggles

*Read in the* I Am Second *book before your next meeting*

Brian "Head" Welch ............... chapter 1

## Want more? See also

# 2.0 second: struggles

## Talk with God

Ask God to help you learn and understand as you discuss the stories in this session.

## The Story

**Watch**: the Brian "Head" Welch film

## Questions:

What do you like or identify with in Brian's story?

What did you not like or find confusing about Brian's story?

What did you learn about people or God through Brian's story?

## for further discussion . . .

What do you like, not like, or identify with in each of the quotes that follow?

"I told myself that I had everything under control, that I could handle it. But I couldn't. My life was just spinning out of control."

—Brian "Head" Welch (*I Am Second*, p. 8)

"I'm weary and burdened, and I need rest for my soul."

—Brian "Head" Welch (*I Am Second*, p. 9)

"One day it will all fail and everyone will be left naked in the face of trouble. But Jesus offers rest in the middle of it all."

—Brian "Head" Welch (*I Am Second*, p. 12)

## The Bible

Read this story together.

> They went across the lake to the region of the Gerasenes. When Jesus got out of the boat, a man with an impure spirit came from the tombs to meet him. This man lived in the tombs, and no one could bind him anymore, not even with a chain. For he had often been chained hand and foot, but he tore the chains apart and broke the irons on his feet. No one was strong enough to subdue him. Night and day among the tombs and in the hills he would cry out and cut himself with stones.

When he saw Jesus from a distance, he ran and fell on his knees in front of him. He shouted at the top of his voice, "What do you want with me, Jesus, Son of the Most High God? In God's name don't torture me!" For Jesus had said to him, "Come out of this man, you impure spirit!"

Then Jesus asked him, "What is your name?"

"My name is Legion," he replied, "for we are many." And he begged Jesus again and again not to send them out of the area.

A large herd of pigs was feeding on the nearby hillside. The demons begged Jesus, "Send us among the pigs; allow us to go into them." He gave them permission, and the impure spirits came out and went into the pigs. The herd, about two thousand in number, rushed down the steep bank into the lake and were drowned.

Those tending the pigs ran off and reported this in the town and countryside, and the people went out to see what had happened. When they came to Jesus, they saw the man who had been possessed by the legion of demons, sitting there, dressed and in his right mind; and they were afraid. Those who had seen it told the people what had happened to the demon-possessed man—and told about the pigs as well. Then the people began to plead with Jesus to leave their region.

As Jesus was getting into the boat, the man who had been demon-possessed begged to go with him. Jesus did not let him, but said, "Go home to your own people and tell them how much the Lord has done for you, and how he has had mercy on you." So the man went away and began to tell in the Decapolis how much Jesus had done for him. And all the people were amazed. (Mark 5:1–20)

## Talk about the Bible

1. What do you like about the story?

2. What do you not like or find confusing about the story?

3. What did you learn about people from the story? Where do you see yourself in the story? What struggles do you face?

4. What did you learn about God from the story?

## Live and Tell

5. How will you live out what you have learned? What is something specific and challenging that you can do practically to live this out?

What can your group do to help you achieve this goal?

6. Whom will you tell about what you have learned? What will you share? You can share the film, the book, the Bible story, or just a summary of something you have learned.

Who will you share it with?

# Next Week—
# Second: Relationships

*Read in the* I Am Second *book before your next meeting*

Want more about relationships?

# 3.0 second: relationships

## Talk with God

Ask God to help you learn and understand as you discuss the stories in this session.

## Checkup

How did your Live and Tell commitments go from the last meeting? What went well? What did not go well? How can the group help you or talk with God for you?

## The Story

**Watch**: the Jeff and Cheryl Scruggs film

## Questions:

What did you like or identify with in Jeff and Cheryl's story?

What did you not like or find confusing about their story?

What did you learn about people or God through their story?

## for further discussion . . .

What do you like, not like, or identify with in each of the quotes below?

"We got married thinking we could complete each other, that we somehow could make each other whole. But I wasn't whole. I felt empty. I was missing something."

—**Cheryl Scruggs (*I Am Second*, p. 98)**

"I was so angry at Cheryl that I couldn't even look at her. I would go over to the house, pick up the girls, and just pray that I wouldn't have to look her in the eye or say anything . . . I blamed Cheryl for everything."

—**Jeff Scruggs (*I Am Second*, p. 102)**

"It was hard for me to imagine how Jeff could forgive me for all the hurt that I had caused."

—**Cheryl Scruggs (*I Am Second*, p. 104)**

# The Bible

Read this story together.

Now the tax collectors and sinners were all gathering around to hear Jesus. But the Pharisees and the teachers of the law muttered, "This man welcomes sinners and eats with them. . . ."

Jesus [answered:] "There was a man who had two sons. The younger one said to his father, 'Father, give me my share of the estate.' So he divided his property between them.

"Not long after that, the younger son got together all he had, set off for a distant country and there squandered his wealth in wild living. After he had spent everything, there was a severe famine in that whole country, and he began to be in need. So he went and hired himself out to a citizen of that country, who sent him to his fields to feed pigs. He longed to fill his stomach with the pods that the pigs were eating, but no one gave him anything.

"When he came to his senses, he said, 'How many of my father's hired servants have food to spare, and here I am starving to death! I will set out and go back to my father and say to him: Father, I have sinned against heaven and against you. I am no longer worthy to be called your son; make me like one of your hired servants.' So he got up and went to his father.

"But while he was still a long way off, his father saw him and was filled with compassion for him; he ran to his son, threw his arms around him and kissed him.

"The son said to him, 'Father, I have sinned against heaven and against you. I am no longer worthy to be called your son.'

"But the father said to his servants, 'Quick! Bring the best robe and put it on him. Put a ring on his finger and sandals on his feet. Bring the fattened calf and kill it. Let's have a feast and celebrate. For this son of mine was dead and is alive again; he was lost and is found.' So they began to celebrate.

"Meanwhile, the older son was in the field. When he came near the house, he heard music and dancing. So he called one of the servants and asked him what was going on. 'Your brother has come,' he replied, 'and your father has killed the fattened calf because he has him back safe and sound.'

"The older brother became angry and refused to go in. So his father went out and pleaded with him. But he answered his father, 'Look! All these years I've been slaving for you and never disobeyed your orders. Yet you never gave me even a young goat so I could celebrate with my friends. But when this son of yours who has squandered your property with prostitutes comes home, you kill the fattened calf for him!'

"'My son,' the father said, 'you are always with me, and everything I have is yours. But we had to celebrate and be glad, because this brother of yours was dead and is alive again; he was lost and is found.'" (Luke 15:1–2, 11–32)

## Talk about the Bible

1. What do you like about the story?

2. What do you not like or find confusing about the story?

3. What did you learn about people from the story? What did you learn about forgiveness through this story?

4. What did you learn about God from the story? How can the father be an image of God in this story?

## Live and Tell

5. How will you live out what you have learned? What is something specific and challenging that you can do practically to live this out?

What can your group do to help you?

6. Who will you tell about what you have learned?

What will you share? You can share the film, the book, the Bible story, or just a summary of something you have learned.

Who will you share it with?

# Next Week—
# Second: Success

*Read in the* I Am Second *book before your next meeting*

## Want more about success?

# 4.0 second: success

## Talk with God

Ask God to help you learn and understand as you discuss the stories in this session.

## Checkup

How did your Live and Tell commitments go from last meeting? What went well? What didn't go well? How can the group help or talk with God for you this coming week?

## The Story

**Watch**: the Brian Sumner film

## Questions:

What did you like or identify with in Brian's story?

What did you not like or find confusing about his story?

What did you learn about people or God through his story?

## for further discussion . . .

What do you like, not like, or identify with in each of the quotes below?

"I came to America to find the American dream, and I found it, but I was miserable and angry. I accomplished more than I ever dreamed of doing . . . but I felt so empty. I was full of anger. I said wicked things to my wife, things I didn't even believe, but I said them because I was so stupid and so mad. The anger was just boiling inside of me."

—Brian Sumner (*I Am Second*, p. 150)

"I knew God was out there. But that was all I knew. Was it Buddha? Is he a Rasta? Was he in Ouija boards and séances? God was just this higher power. He was the guy at the pearly gates at the end of life."

—Brian Sumner (*I Am Second*, p. 151)

"God is real. I couldn't believe that I had lived my whole life not knowing that God was real, that I could meet him. I couldn't believe that people didn't know this."

—Brian Sumner (*I Am Second*, p. 153)

# The Bible

Read this story together.

> Jesus entered Jericho and was passing through. A man was there by the name of Zacchaeus ["Zack-key-us"]; he was a chief tax collector and was wealthy. He wanted to see who Jesus was, but because he was short he could not see over the crowd. So he ran ahead and climbed a sycamore-fig tree to see him, since Jesus was coming that way.
>
> When Jesus reached the spot, he looked up and said to him, "Zacchaeus, come down immediately. I must stay at your house today." So he came down at once and welcomed him gladly.
>
> All the people saw this and began to mutter, "He has gone to be the guest of a sinner."
>
> But Zacchaeus stood up and said to the Lord, "Look, Lord! Here and now I give half of my possessions to the poor, and if I have cheated anybody out of anything, I will pay back four times the amount."
>
> Jesus said to him, "Today salvation has come to this house, because this man, too, is a son of Abraham. For the Son of Man came to seek and to save the lost." (Luke 19:1–10)

## Talk about the Bible

1. What do you like about the story?

2. What do you not like or find confusing about the story? Why were Jesus' actions shocking to the crowd?

3. What did you learn about people from the story?

4. What did you learn about God from the story? How did Jesus respond to "sinners" in this story?

## Live and Tell

5. How will you live out what you have learned? What is something specific and challenging that you can do practically to live this out?

   What can your group do to help you?

6. Who will you tell about what you have learned?

What will you share? You can share the film, the book, the Bible story, or just a summary of something you have learned.

Who will you share it with?

# Next Week—
# Who Is First?

*Read in the* I Am Second *book before your next meeting*

## Want more about who is first?

# 5.0 who is first?

## Talk with God

Ask God to help you learn and understand as you discuss the stories in this session.

## Checkup

How did your Live and Tell commitments go from last meeting? What went well? What didn't go well? How can the group help or talk with God for you this coming week?

## The Story

**Watch**: the Tamara Jolee film

## Questions:

What did you like or identify with in Tamara's story?

What did you not like or find confusing about her story?

What did you learn about people or God through her story?

## for further discussion . . .

What do you like, not like, or identify with in each of the quotes below?

"I'm not just living anymore, I'm surviving . . . People tell me now, 'Wow! You are doing so well.' But they weren't with me during the sleepless nights, with medical steroids roaring through my system . . . I was sick, real sick."

—Tamara Jolee (*I Am Second*, p. 177)

"I finally realized that God wanted more than my religious commitment; he wanted me. He wanted to sit next to me in class, to walk with me through life. God wanted to be my friend . . . There were still battles to face, but having a relationship with God meant that there was always someone to lean on."

—Tamara Jolee (*I Am Second*, p. 177)

"I never know if tomorrow will be my last. But if I do die tomorrow, or even if I die today, I'm completely and truly at peace with that. I know I'm not alone."

—Tamara Jolee (*I Am Second*, p. 178)

# The Bible

Read this story together.

Background: A messenger came to Jesus with news that Lazarus, one of Jesus' closest friends, was on the brink of death. Jesus had healed many people prior to this. But he did not heal Lazarus. Instead, he waited and did nothing, and Lazarus died. Days later, Jesus finally arrived at this man's village, only to be met by Lazarus's two sisters, Mary and Martha, who were heartbroken and confused as to why Jesus did not heal their brother and his dear friend.

"Lord," Martha said to Jesus, "if you had been here, my brother would not have died. But I know that even now God will give you whatever you ask."

Jesus said to her, "Your brother will rise again."

Martha answered, "I know he will rise again in the resurrection at the last day."

Jesus said to her, "I am the resurrection and the life. The one who believes in me will live, even though they die; and whoever lives by believing in me will never die. Do you believe this?"

"Yes, Lord," she replied, "I believe that you are the Messiah, the Son of God, who is to come into the world. . . ."

When Mary reached the place where Jesus was and saw him, she fell at his feet and said, "Lord, if you had been here, my brother would not have died."

When Jesus saw her weeping, and the Jews who had come along with her also weeping, he was deeply moved in spirit and troubled. "Where have you laid him?" he asked.

"Come and see, Lord," they replied.

Jesus wept.

Then the Jews said, "See how he loved him!"

But some of them said, "Could not he who opened the eyes of the blind man have kept this man from dying?"

Jesus, once more deeply moved, came to the tomb. It was a cave with a stone laid across the entrance. "Take away the stone," he said.

"But, Lord," said Martha, the sister of the dead man, "by this time there is a bad odor, for he has been there four days."

Then Jesus said, "Did I not tell you that if you believe, you will see the glory of God?"

So they took away the stone. Then Jesus looked up and said, "Father, I thank you that you have heard me. I knew that you always hear me, but I said this for the benefit of the people standing here, that they may believe that you sent me."

When he had said this, Jesus called in a loud voice, "Lazarus, come out!" The dead man came out, his hands and feet wrapped with strips of linen, and a cloth around his face.

Jesus said to them, "Take off the grave clothes and let him go."

Therefore many of the Jews who had come to visit Mary, and had seen what Jesus did, believed in him. But some of them went to the Pharisees and told them what Jesus had done. (John 11:21–27, 32–46)

## Talk about the Bible

1. What do you like or identify with in the story?

2. What do you not like or find confusing about the story? Why do you think Jesus waited to go see Lazarus?

3. What did you learn about people from the story? What does this story teach about life and death?

4. What did you learn about Jesus from the story? What did Jesus claim about his power over death? What do you think about this claim?

## Live and Tell

5. How will you live out what you have learned? What is something specific and challenging that you can do practically to live this out?

What can your group do to help you?

6. Who will you tell about what you have learned?

What will you share? You can share the film, the book, the Bible story, or just a summary of something you have learned.

Who will you share it with?

7. Are you interested in learning what it means to believe in Jesus and his claims, and to follow him? To learn how, see the "How Do I Become Second?" section in the back of this discussion guide.

# 6.0 tell your story

## Talk with God

Ask God to help you learn and understand as you discuss the stories in this session.

## Checkup

How did your Live and Tell commitments go from last meeting? What went well? What didn't go well? How can the group help or talk with God for you this coming week?

## The Story

**Watch**: the Share Your Story film

## Questions:

What did you like or identify with in these stories?

What did each story have in common?

# The Bible

Read this story together.

Background: Jesus and his followers entered a land called Samaria. Jews generally had racial and historical prejudices against this country and the people that occupied it and refused any contact with them. But Jesus entered the land anyway and conversed with a woman. This woman, along with her people, had for many generations waited for one called the Anointed, who they believed would rescue the world.

> Now he had to go through Samaria. So he came to a town in Samaria called Sychar, near the plot of ground Jacob had given to his son Joseph. Jacob's well was there, and Jesus, tired as he was from the journey, sat down by the well. It was about noon.
>
> When a Samaritan woman came to draw water, Jesus said to her, "Will you give me a drink?" (His disciples had gone into the town to buy food.)
>
> The Samaritan woman said to him, "You are a Jew and I am a Samaritan woman. How can you ask me for a drink?" (For Jews do not associate with Samaritans.)
>
> Jesus answered her, "If you knew the gift of God and who it is that asks you for a drink, you would have asked him and he would have given you living water."

"Sir," the woman said, "you have nothing to draw with and the well is deep. Where can you get this living water? Are you greater than our father Jacob, who gave us the well and drank from it himself, as did also his sons and his livestock?"

Jesus answered, "Everyone who drinks this water will be thirsty again, but whoever drinks the water I give them will never thirst. Indeed, the water I give them will become in them a spring of water welling up to eternal life."

The woman said to him, "Sir, give me this water so that I won't get thirsty and have to keep coming here to draw water."

He told her, "Go, call your husband and come back."

"I have no husband," she replied.

Jesus said to her, "You are right when you say you have no husband. The fact is, you have had five husbands, and the man you now have is not your husband. What you have just said is quite true."

"Sir," the woman said, "I can see that you are a prophet. . . ."

The woman said, "I know that Messiah" (called Christ) "is coming. When he comes, he will explain everything to us."

Then Jesus declared, "I, the one speaking to you—I am he."

Just then his disciples returned and were surprised to find him talking with a woman. But no one asked, "What do you want?" or "Why are you talking with her?"

Then, leaving her water jar, the woman went back to the town and said to the people, "Come, see a man who told me everything I ever did. Could this be the Messiah?" They came out of the town and made their way toward him. . . .

Many of the Samaritans from that town believed in him because of the woman's testimony, "He told me everything I ever did." So when the Samaritans came to him, they urged him to stay with them, and he stayed two days. And because of his words many more became believers.

They said to the woman, "We no longer believe just because of what you said; now we have heard for ourselves, and we know that this man really is the Savior of the world." (John 4:4–19, 25–30, 39–42)

## Talk about the Bible

1. What do you like or identify with in the story? What was unusual about Jesus talking with this woman?

2. What do you not like or find confusing about the story?

3. What did you learn about people from the story? How was this woman's story used to transform her village?

4. What did you learn about Jesus from the story? How did Jesus use this woman to reach her village?

## Live and Tell

5. What is your story? If you had been at that well and you had met Jesus, what story would you share with your village? How would you tell your story if you were sitting in the white chair?

Think of a big moment you have had with God. Your story may be about the time you became a believer. It may be another moment in your life. But think of a time when you interacted with or came to a new understanding of God.

What were you like before this moment?

What happened to cause this change?

What changed as a result of this moment?

Take turns sharing your stories with the people in your group.
Practice telling your story.

6. To whom will you tell your story?

The woman at the well had a village of people that needed to hear her story. In a sense, we all have a village, a group or network of people in our lives that need to hear our story as well. Who is in your village that you could begin sharing your story with?

## Start a new group?

Each week, you have been challenged to tell others about what you have been learning. You may have talked with friends, neighbors, coworkers, or classmates. Perhaps many of the people in your "village" have begun to see what you are learning. Who has shown interest? Who do you think might want to learn more? Who can you invite to start a new group with you? Take the challenge, and help your friends and family experience the power of real stories and changing lives.

 # Leader's Guide

# how to lead your group

Keep these principles in mind as you lead your group. Use the S.E.C.O.N.D acrostic to help you remember these points.

**S**tories and Small. Encourage people to tell their stories. Listen to the stories of others. Then discuss stories from the Bible. Keep your group small (between 2 and 8 people) to maximize impact and allow everyone to discuss these stories.

**E**veryone contributes. Each person in your group should feel the freedom to contribute to the group. Help people learn how to grow by modeling these things and helping them do these things themselves: (a) tell others about Jesus, (b) learn the Bible, (c) talk with God, (d) help and encourage others, and (e) endure hard times.

**C**onsider everyone a potential leader. View everyone as potential leaders, both before and after they trust Jesus. Give people opportunities to lead if they continue to obey and progress. We recommend that leaders be unpaid and not required to have formal training. All leaders should, however, have a mentor or be accountable to someone else.

**O**bedience-based, not just knowledge-focused. Make a "Live and Tell" commitment every time you meet. Allow the Holy Spirit to guide people in the life changes they need to make as you do the "Live and Tell" questions. At the beginning of each meeting, review the previous meeting's commitments.

**N**ew groups rather than big groups. As people share with others, encourage them not to invite the new people to your group, but instead start a new group themselves. Meet in homes or neutral places, such as coffee shops or a park. Meet with new group leaders as a coach, and encourage them to do the same for others. Stay connected for ongoing training and accountability.

**D**iscuss and discover. Focus on the Bible. Trust the Holy Spirit to help each person discover the meaning of Scripture as your group discusses it. Be prepared to guide the discussion to keep everyone focused on the plain meaning of the Bible passage rather than any unusual interpretations, outside philosophies, or strange worldviews. Lead through asking questions rather than lecture. If questions arise for which you don't have answers, offer to help find those answers.

# helps

For training films, free downloads, and other bonus content, register at **iamsecond.com/bonuscontent**.

## 1.0 Your Story

*Be sure to review the "Before you Start" section with your group before beginning this session. It is important that everyone understand the basics of how this group works.*

**Summary**: Encourage your group to openly share where they are in life and in their spiritual journeys with God. At this point, there are no right or wrong answers. There are no good stories or bad stories. And there is no room for judgment and criticism. People should be accepted and welcomed into the group from wherever they are in life.

As a leader, you must model the kind of openness and acceptance that this group needs. When you share your story, make sure you do not appear to be the perfect saint. Be honest, raw, and even vulnerable so that your group sees that you have not arrived at perfection either, and that you, too, need to continue to grow spiritually. This also means that when you hear the stories of others, you do not judge or criticize. Thank each person who shares a story.

The time to provide answers, spiritual guidance, and the message of Jesus will come. But this meeting is not it. This meeting is a time to get to know each other and to see where everyone is spiritually.

**Introduction**: Allow everyone time for a short introduction. This is especially important if everyone in the group does not already know each other. This should not take more than a few minutes.

**Film**: The Josh Hamilton or Michelle Aguilar films are suggested for this meeting.

**Your Story**: This is your group's chance to tell their I am Second stories. The depth and openness of these stories will vary from group to group. However, openness encourages more openness, so don't be afraid to be the first person to open up to the group.

Be sensitive to allow each person to share what he or she feels comfortable sharing. Some will need more time before they can share deeper issues. Others may need to be cut short to allow everyone time to talk about their stories. Use your discretion as you guide the group through this time.

The questions under "Your Story" are meant as guideposts, not mandatory questions. Encourage people to answer the questions they are willing to answer in the process of telling their stories.

**Next Session**: The next session will discuss the Brian "Head" Welch story and will address the issue of struggles. Encourage your group to read the Brian Welch chapter in the *I Am Second* book before your next meeting.

## 2.0 Second: Struggles

**Summary**: Everyone faces struggles, those nagging habits that refuse to retreat. Some may be obvious; some may not. Some are secret; some can't be hidden. But none of them should be faced alone. In this session, Brian "Head" Welch shares his journey with his struggles, his addictions to drugs and alcohol, and the maelstrom that swept around him in his climb to the top. He, like another man who encountered Jesus in the book of Mark, found that healing comes through becoming Second.

**Talk with God**. Take a few moments and talk with God about helping your group through this session. Ask him to help you as you study and discuss. Ask him to help you live out the things you learn.

## The Story

Use the Brian Welch film and his story in the *I Am Second* book as a starting place for your discussion about struggles. The questions provided are specifically designed to be broad and open-ended in nature. This allows your group the freedom to discuss the specific points and issues most relevant for your group. We recommend not adding questions, especially ones that are overly specific, as this tends to hinder meaningful discussion.

*Primary themes*. Brian's story may lead your group to discuss several important and common struggles, including drug and alcohol addiction, family issues (marital or parental), or even success and materialism. Encourage your group to discuss the aspects of this story that seem most relevant.

*Further discussion*. If your group has additional time or is struggling to deeply engage with the story, use the quotes we've provided and the questions that go with them as a point of reference to keep things moving.

## The Bible

Read the Bible story together as a group. Have different people read each part of the story.

*Talk about the Bible.*

Below are common observations or lessons that come from this story. While your group does not need to discuss every point highlighted below, it is important that your group catch the big ideas. As possible, guide and lead your group to these big ideas through questions rather than direct teaching.

1. *What do you like?* Fear and rejection, hardship and struggles were common experiences for this man. But Jesus still cared for him and wanted to see him healed. He didn't bring judgment or trouble; he brought a solution. Jesus brought what no one else could, a new life. The price for this healing was an entire herd of pigs, a small fortune at the time. But for Jesus one life was worth the cost.

2. *What do you not like or find confusing?* The passage highlights the difficulties that many will face as they confront their struggles. The community knew about this man and the issues he dealt with. But when healing came, fear, not celebration, was the reaction. There were no parades, no parties, no moving speeches, just a request for Jesus to leave. The people cared more about their lost livestock and the possibility of losing more than they did about the man who had been given a second chance.

3. *What does this teach about people?* No struggle, no addiction, no problem, no issue is bigger than Jesus. He can handle the worst of our messes. Some are tempted to think that some things are beyond forgiveness, that some things can't be changed; but Jesus proves otherwise in this story.

4. *What does this teach about God?* There is no one God cannot save. Jesus took a crazed, possessed man who was beyond help by anyone else and saved him. Then he took that man and sent him back to his own people to tell the story of God's mercy.

## Live and Tell

*Live.* Challenge the people in your group to take practical and challenging steps toward facing a struggle in their lives. For some this will mean working on a broken relationship; for others it may mean joining a recovery program. Whatever decision each person makes, encourage everyone to list a date and time for the next action step. Offer prayer for people as they make decisions.

*Tell.* Help participants write out what they have learned and identify someone they can share those lessons with in the coming week.

**Next Session**: The next session will discuss the Jeff and Cheryl Scruggs story and will address the issue of relationships. Encourage your group to read the Scruggs chapter in the *I Am Second* book before your next meeting.

# 3.0 Second: Relationships

**Summary**: Relationships can be both fragile and powerful. They offer the greatest hope for love, acceptance, and meaning, but also the greatest risk for pain. The Scruggses discuss their journey from love, to divorce, and back to love again, and all the pain and difficulties that occurred along the way. Jesus tells another story about a father whose son rebels and wastes his father's wealth, only to crawl back in desperation. The need and power of forgiveness shines through both stories.

**Talk with God**. Take a few moments and ask God to help your group as you discuss these stories.

**Checkup**. Review the Live and Tell commitments from your previous meeting. Be sure to have a written record of everyone's action plans. Talk about what went well, what didn't go well, and what can be improved on in the future. Holding people accountable for their commitments is a key to spiritual growth. Love people enough to help them grow, and set the expectation that the Live and Tell commitments are vital portions of every session.

## The Story

Use the Jeff and Cheryl Scruggs film and their story in the *I Am Second* book as a starting place for your discussion about relationships. The questions provided are specifically designed to be broad and open-ended in nature. This allows your group the freedom to discuss the specific points and issues most relevant for your group.

*Primary themes.* The Scruggses' story may lead your group to discuss many relationship-related topics, including forgiveness, honesty, finances, conflict resolution, divorce, and parenting. Encourage your group to discuss the aspects of this story that seem most relevant.

*Further discussion.* If your group has additional time or is struggling to deeply engage with the story, use these quotes and the questions that go with them as a point of reference to keep things moving.

## The Bible.

Read the Bible story together as a group. Have different people read each part of the story.

*Talk about the Bible.*

1. *What do you like?* The runaway son expected his father to disown him. At most, the son hoped his father would treat him as a servant. He knew he had dishonored his family and wasted his father's inheritance and that he deserved nothing more. But when he returned, his father was overwhelmed with joy. He threw his lost son a party, showered him with gifts, and welcomed him back with complete forgiveness.

2. *What do you not like or find confusing?* The brother did not share his father's sense of forgiveness. When he saw his brother had returned, he felt jealousy and anger, not love. He couldn't see past his brother's failures. Jesus told this story to religious leaders who apparently were likewise unable to forgive or believe that people could change.

3. *What does this teach about people?* Without forgiveness, love will fade into anger and jealousy. The father could have chosen to let anger be his response, but instead, he allowed forgiveness to reunite him with a repentant son. Unfortunately, many people are like the religious leaders and the brother in the story and cannot allow old hurts, past sins, or broken people to experience the forgiveness that everyone needs at some point in life.

4. *What does this teach about God?* The religious leaders of the day avoided contact with "sinners." Rather than using the Bible as a message of hope and forgiveness, they used it as a weapon of judgment. Jesus came to correct their misconceptions and spent large portions of his time and ministry with notorious sinners. Sin is truly a deadly reality, but Jesus came to show people the way back to the Father, the way to forgiveness.

## Live and Tell

*Live.* Challenge everyone in your group to take practical and challenging steps toward giving and accepting forgiveness. This may mean starting a relationship with God for some; for others this may mean taking steps to forgive old friends or family. Whatever decision each person makes, encourage everyone to list a date and time for the next action step. Offer prayer for people as they make decisions.

*Tell.* Help participants write out what they have learned and identify someone they can share those lessons with in the coming week.

**Next Session**: The next session will discuss the Brian Sumner story and will address the issue of success. Encourage your group to read the Brian Sumner chapter in the *I Am Second* book before your next meeting.

# 4.0 Second: Success

**Summary**: Money. Power. Fame. Success by most measurements. But is it enough? Brian Sumner tells of his trip to the top and the anger and emptiness he found while there. Zacchaeus found similar success. He had money, good connections, was a high-ranking official. But he, too, found that Jesus had something to offer that could not be bought with money or influence. In these stories, watch Jesus challenge how success is defined.

**Talk with God**. Take a few moments and ask God to help you as you discuss the stories in this session.

**Checkup**. Review the Live and Tell commitments from your previous meeting. Be sure to have a written record of everyone's action plans. Talk about what went well, what didn't go well, and what can be improved on in the future. Holding people accountable for their commitments is a key to spiritual growth. Love people enough to help them grow, and set the expectation that the Live and Tell commitments are vital portions of every session.

## The Story

Use the Brian Sumner film and his story in the *I Am Second* book as a starting place for your discussion about success. The questions provided are specifically designed to be broad and open-ended in nature. This allows your group the freedom to discuss the specific points and issues most relevant for your group. If you choose to add other questions, avoid yes/no questions or questions with obvious or simple answers, as they tend to discourage meaningful discussion.

*Primary themes.* Brian Sumner's story may lead your group to discuss several success-related topics, including, money, career, fame, power, influence, materialism, and the effects these can have on relationships. Encourage your group to discuss the aspects of this story that seem most relevant.

*Further discussion.* If your group has additional time or is struggling to deeply engage with the story, use these quotes and the questions that go with them as a point of reference to keep things moving.

## The Bible

Read the Bible story together as a group. Have different people read each part of the story.

*Talk about the Bible*

1. *What do you like?* Jesus went against the cultural norms of his day and associated with those considered to be terrible people. He even made his associations with these people public by announcing his intentions to spend time at Zacchaeus's house. Zacchaeus was truly changed through the time he spent with Jesus. This wealthy tax collector gave half of his possessions to the poor and swore to right all his wrongs.

2. *What do you not like or find confusing?* Cheating people was a common occurrence for tax collectors of the day. The government gave them small salaries, which were almost always subsidized by tax collectors overtaxing people and then pocketing the difference for their own gain. This contributed to the hatred that many people felt toward those in Zacchaeus's line of work. When Zacchaeus chose to give half his money to the poor and then pay back fourfold everyone he may have cheated, that would have been a substantial portion, if not the entirety, of his wealth. His actions would have been in huge contrast to the actions of his colleagues.

3. *What did you learn about people?* Zacchaeus found that success and wealth lose their value. The message and person of Jesus were so convincing and so powerful that someone labeled a notorious sinner would completely change his life on meeting him. Brian Sumner illustrated the same truth, that when a person meets Jesus, all the wealth, power, and influence in the world are meaningless in comparison.

4. *What did you learn about God?* The passage does not detail Zacchaeus's sins. He is labeled a notorious sinner, and his career choice all but guarantees this to be true. But despite his failings and despite his greed or poor choices, Jesus still loved him and wanted to see his life change for the better. Unlike the crowd that witnessed this episode, Jesus offered hope, forgiveness, and something greater than money. As illustrated through Brian Sumner's story, Jesus is still making the same offer.

## Live and Tell

*Live.* Challenge everyone in your group to take practical and challenging steps toward using their money, power, and success for God and for others. Changes in career goals, financial plans, or even giving habits all can be helpful steps in rethinking success. Whatever decision each person makes, encourage everyone to list a date and time for the next action step. Offer prayer for people as they make decisions.

*Tell.* Help participants write out what they have learned and identify someone they can share those lessons with in the coming week.

**Next Session**: The next session will discuss the Tamara Jolee story and will address the topic of death. Encourage your group to read Tamara's chapter in the *I Am Second* book before your next meeting.

# 5.0 Who Is First?

**Summary**: Tamara Jolee faced death. Stage 4 cancer with no cure. She learned to be at peace with death. Lazarus, too, became sick and later even died. His family had to grapple with the reality of his departing and the hope of seeing him again. But they all found their peace and hope only through Jesus.

**Talk with God**. Take a few moments and ask God to help you as you discuss the stories in this session.

**Checkup**. Review the Live and Tell commitments from your previous meeting. Be sure to have a written record of everyone's action plans. Talk about what went well, what didn't go well, and what can be improved on in the future. Holding people accountable for their commitments is a key to spiritual growth. Love people enough to help them grow, and set the expectation that the Live and Tell commitments are vital portions of every session.

## The Story

Use the Tamara Jolee film and her story in the *I Am Second* book as a starting place for your discussion about who is first. The questions provided are specifically designed to be broad and open-ended in nature. This allows your group the freedom to discuss the specific points and issues most relevant for your group. If you choose to add other questions, avoid yes/no questions or questions with obvious or simple answers, as they tend to discourage meaningful discussion.

*Primary themes*. Tamara Jolee's story may lead your group to discuss the topics of who Jesus claimed to be, death and what comes next, and what it means to become Second. Encourage your group to discuss the aspects of this story that seem most relevant. Learn more in the "How Do I Become Second?" section of this participant guide.

*Further discussion*. If your group has additional time or is struggling to deeply engage with the story, use these quotes and the questions that go with them as a point of reference to keep things moving.

## The Bible

Read the Bible story together as a group. Have different people read each part of the story.

*Talk about the Bible.*

1. *What do you like?* Jesus identified with the pain and suffering that death caused in Lazarus's family. Jesus wept with them. But he also provided hope. He showed he had the power to resurrect the dead and claimed to be the source of life itself. And while Lazarus would one day die again, Jesus promised to resurrect all who believed in him and give them life that never ends.

2. *What do you not like or find confusing?* If Jesus was truly as sad as he seemed to be, by weeping at Lazarus's death, then why did he allow him to die in the first place? It seems that in this particular situation, Jesus had a lesson he wanted to teach. He wanted to show that those who believed in him would have eternal life, that through him death would have no permanent hold. Raising Lazarus from the dead demonstrated that truth.

God continues to allow people to become sick, face hardships, and even die. At times, he seems to be teaching something specific to those involved. But most times, he simply allows the world to take its course. Humanity at large has chosen to live without God. Death and pain are signs that he has granted that choice so that one day some may realize their need for him.

3. *What did you learn about people?* This world and this life will have pain, even death. Bad things will happen to good people. While God often rewards good deeds or good people in this life, his ultimate and absolute reward, the reward that cannot be taken away or lost, comes after this life.

4. *What did you learn about God?* While pain and death will always be a part of this world, Jesus offers a solution. For those who believe in him, in who he is and what he did, he offers life that never ends in a new future world without any pain. Jesus offered Lazarus a temporary solution, but he did so to remind his followers of the never-ending life he offers to those who follow him.

## Live and Tell

*Live.* Challenge everyone in your group to take practical and challenging steps toward confronting the big question in life. If Jesus is really first, what needs to change? If someone chooses to accept Jesus as First, set aside time after the group to walk that person through the "How Do I Become Second?" section in the back of this participant guide.

*Tell.* Help participants write out what they have learned and identify someone they can share those lessons with in the coming week.

**Next Session**: The next session will discuss how to tell your story. As the group has gone through the Live and Tell each week, they have been telling others about what they are learning. Next week's session will help them go one step further by telling their own stories. Encourage your group to begin thinking about how they might tell their stories to the people in their lives.

## 6.0 Tell Your Story

**Summary**: Everyone has a story. And these stories are meant to be shared. This session is all about learning how to do just that.

**Talk with God.** Take a few moments and ask God to help you as you discuss the stories in this session.

**Checkup**. Review the Live and Tell commitments from your previous meeting. Be sure to have a written record of everyone's action plans. Talk about what went well, what didn't go well, and what can be improved on in the future. Holding people accountable for their commitments is a key to spiritual growth. Love people enough to help them grow, and set the expectation that the Live and Tell commitments are vital portions of every session.

## Share Your Story Film

This film shows people whose spiritual journeys were radically changed when someone shared with them his or her own story or the message of Jesus. While each story is different, they all demonstrate the power of telling your story.

## The Bible

Read the Bible story together as a group. Have different people read each part of the story.

*Talk about the Bible.*

1. *What do you like?* Jesus did the uncomfortable. He went to a place and talked with a woman to whom few would have dared to speak. He broke cultural rules and shocked even his closest followers. But he did it because he knew that

woman needed God, and he knew she would have a story to tell. And sure enough, her witness, her story, brought the whole village to Jesus.

2. *What do you not like?* The woman at the well did not immediately understand what Jesus was trying to tell her. Even after Jesus offered living water, she had several questions before she understood who he was and what he was talking about.

3. *What did you learn about people?* When she returned to her village, the woman shared a simple message. First, she summarized her experience with Jesus. She explained that she realized that he was more than just a man after he told her everything that she had done. Second, she asked a question that piqued the interest of her village. She did not condemn them or preach at them. She simply asked what they thought about Jesus. This shows a beautiful example of how to start spiritual conversations with people.

4. *What did you learn about God?* God has given everyone a story. Some are full of hardship and pain; others are about relationships or careers; everyone has a different story. But when Jesus comes into a life, that story becomes uniquely powerful and is meant to be shared.

## Live and Tell

*Live.* Take time to let everyone write out, share, and practice telling their stories. These stories should be short, just a few minutes long. It does not have to be a person's whole life story. It can be just the highlights of his or her spiritual journey or one episode of that journey. But give everyone a chance to practice their stories.

*Tell.* The woman at the well had a village of people that needed to hear her story. In a sense, we all have a village, a group or network of people in our lives who need to hear our story as well. Who is in your village that you could begin sharing your story with?

## Start a new group?

Discuss next steps for the group. Who is interested in starting a new group? Who would like to continue with this group?

# next steps

## Option 1: Same Participant's Guide, New Group.

Have you been inspired? Have you been challenged? Have the stories of *I Am Second* moved you? Then consider bringing these stories to your friends and family by going through this same discussion guide with them.

- ➔ *Get the Materials.* Go to your local bookstore, visit **thomasnelson.com**, or talk with your group leader about getting materials for your group.

- ➔ *Find Interested People.* Each week your group has used the Live and Tell as an opportunity to share what you are learning with others. Who has seemed interested in learning more? Who do you think would want to start a group with you? Share the *I Am Second* stories using the book or the films and ask people if they would be interested in starting a group with you. And remember these groups are not just for Christians.

- ⊛ *Pick a Time and Place.* Find a time and place that works for everyone.
- ⊛ *Stay Connected.* Stay connected with your current group leader for ongoing support and guidance.

## Option 2: Keep Meeting

Want to keep meeting? Great! Use the "Go Further" list on the next page or go to **iamsecond.com/groups** for more group materials and tools.

# go further

This discussion guide has walked you through just a few of the stories in *I Am Second: Real Stories. Changing Lives.* To go further use the list below to keep the discussion flowing. You can use the same format for each meeting. Discuss the story from the book, discuss the story from the Bible passage listed below, and discuss Live and Tells. For films of each of these stories go to **iamsecond.com**.

Brian "Head" Welch (on the DVD)
"The Possessed Man"–Mark 5:1–20

Daniel Montenegro
"Lame Man Forgiven"—Mark 2:1–12

Josh Hamilton
"I Do What I Hate"—Romans 7:14–25

Michelle Aguilar
"Woman and Daughter Healed"—Luke 8:40–56

Nate Larkin
"Jewish Hypocrites"—Matthew 23:1–15

Karen Green
"Gift of Sinful Woman"—Luke 7:36–50

Michael W. Smith
"Least of These"—Matthew 25:31–46

Shannon Culpepper
"Woman at the Well"—John 4:5–19, 25–30, 39–42

Jeff and Cheryl Scruggs (on the DVD)
"Story of Runaway Son"—Luke 15:1–2, 11–32

Vitor Belfort
"Story of Soils"—Luke 8:1–15

Ken Hutcherson
"Forgiving Debts"—Matthew 18:21–35

Whispering Danny
"The Way"—John 14:1–14

Brian Sumner (on the DVD)
"Tax Collector Gives"—Luke 19:1–10

Chris Plekenpol
"Jesus' Death"—Luke 23:26–43

Tamara Jolee (on the DVD)
"Dead Made Alive"—John 11:21–27, 32–46

Bradie James
"Greatest Servant"—John 13:1–17

Bethany Hamilton
"Healing"—Luke 8:40–56

Laura Klock
"Questions"—John 3:1–21

Sam Bradford
"Greatest Commandment"—Luke 10:25–37

Norm Miller
"First Will Be Last"—Mark 10:17–31

# how do I become second?

Becoming second means recognizing God is first. It means believing and trusting in Jesus and accepting who he is and what he did. The stories of *I Am Second* illustrate the peace, purpose, and freedom that many people experienced when they made the decision to be second. But the thread that holds each of these stories together is not so much what they got out of their experiences but where they began.

They each began by understanding that they were broken people. They each believed that they were sinners. Nobody escapes the weaknesses of being human. No one is without failures and mistakes, pride or selfishness. Everyone fails to love as they should.

These sins or failures separate people from God. They also bring a punishment. According to Romans 6:23, the wages of sin is death. Because of sin, everyone will face judgment when they die. "People are destined to die once, and after that to face judgment" (Heb. 9:27). God does not judge whether someone did more right than wrong. Perfection is the standard. Sin at any level, any amount, makes one guilty. Even in the present-day world, a person who commits a crime is not judged by whether he has done more good than he has wrong. He is judged on whether or not he committed the crime. Those who depend on their own good works are destined to spend eternity separated from God in hell.

But God offers forgiveness for all these sins. He offers forgiveness through faith in Jesus. It starts with an admission of guilt, a change of mind, a willingness to start going God's way instead of going our own way. It is admitting we are full of sin and in desperate need of help. But it is not just any help we must look for; it is Jesus' help. It is Jesus we need. It is his message and sacrifice that we must accept and believe to experience forgiveness and a relationship with God. It is about faith in the God of the Bible and in his Son, Jesus, who came and died for the sins of the world.

So who is this Jesus?

**Jesus is first**. It's not about us. It's not about our good deeds or religion. It's about who Jesus is and what he did. "For what we preach is not ourselves, but Jesus Christ as Lord, and ourselves as your servants for Jesus' sake" (2 Cor. 4:5). It's about Jesus, always and fully God, who came to earth and was born a baby in full humanity, who later died on a cross for our sins, and who raised to life on the third day.

**Jesus died to forgive our sins**. The message of Jesus is simple and is summarized in 1 Corinthians 15:1–4: "Now, brothers and sisters, I want to remind you of the gospel I preached to you, which you received and on which you have taken your stand. By this gospel you are saved, if you hold firmly to the word I preached to you . . . that Christ died for our sins according to the Scriptures, that he was buried, that he was raised on the third day according to the Scriptures." Without the death of Jesus, there would be no forgiveness of sins.

**Jesus rose from the dead**. The foundation of our faith is not our personal story. The foundation of our faith is a historic event: the resurrection of Jesus. Paul wrote, "And if Christ has not been raised, your faith is futile; you are still in your sins" (1 Cor. 15:17).

**We are saved by God's grace, not by good works**. We do not earn forgiveness. It is a gift. "Now to the one who works, wages are not credited as a gift but as an obligation. However, to the one who does not work but trusts God who justifies the ungodly, their faith is credited as righteousness" (Rom. 4:4–5). God expects our behavior and lives to change, but the change does not save us.

**We are saved by grace, through faith**. This gift is received through believing. "For it is by grace you have been saved, through faith—and this is not from yourselves, it is the gift of God—not by works, so that no one can boast" (Eph. 2:8–9).

If you want to be second, if you believe in Jesus, who he is and what he did, take a moment right now and tell him. Tell him what you believe, and ask him for forgiveness. Ask God to make you a part of his family.

## What now?

If you have made that commitment to be second, trusted in Jesus, and accepted his forgiveness, here are some next steps for you to do. To learn more about each of these topics, download the *Jesus Says* and the *Jesus Also Says* discussion guides at **iamsecond.com/groups**.

**Be baptized**. Show the world you follow Jesus.

"Go and make disciples . . . baptizing them in the name of the Father and of the Son and of the Holy Spirit."

**–Jesus, Matthew 28:19**

**Love God. Love people**. Live the life of second.

"Love the Lord your God with all your heart. . . . Love your neighbor as yourself."

> **–Jesus, Luke 10:27**

**Commemorate Jesus**. Get with other believers and remember the death of Jesus.

"Whenever you eat this bread and drink this cup, you proclaim the Lord's death until he comes."

> **–Paul, 1 Corinthians 11:26**

**Talk with God**. This is a relationship. God wants to hear from you.

"This . . . is how you should pray."

> **–Jesus, Matthew 6:9**

(For more help download our Prayer Journal at **iamsecond.com /groups**.)

**Give**. Your money, time, and talents. Help the poor. Reach the lost.

"It is more blessed to give than to receive."
**–Jesus, Acts 20:35**

**Make disciples**. Teach others what God has taught you.

"Go and make disciples . . . teaching them to obey everything I have commanded you."
**–Jesus, Matthew 28:19–20**

Learn more about any of these topics by downloading the *Jesus Says* and *Jesus Also Says* discussion guides at **iamsecond.com/groups**.

I Am Second team content contributors to the *I Am Second: Real Stories. Changing Lives* participant's guide include:

Writer...............................Doug Bender

Editor...............................Mike Jorgensen

Creative Design ...............Kristin Baxter, Fernando Gonzalez

Photography....................Stanley Tongai, Trey Hill

For training films, free downloads, sermon outlines, and other bonus content, register your group or church at **iamsecond.com/bonuscontent**.

Additional *I Am Second* participant guides and DVDs of I Am Second films can be found at your local bookstore, **thomasnelson.com**, or **iamsecondstore.com**. For more information on other I Am Second products, ministry opportunities, and how to get involved, e-mail us at:

**connect@iamsecond.com**

I am Second®

214.440.1101

**iamsecond.com**